$4.99

DK

CRAFTY
IDEAS FOR
PARTIES

Many thanks to the children of Richmond House School, Headingley, Leeds for their ideas for games, party food, help and fun. I hope you continue having wonderful parties.

Published in Great Britain in 1993 by
Exley Publications Ltd, 16 Chalk Hill,
Watford, Herts WD1 4BN, United Kingdom.

Published in the USA in 1993 by
Exley Giftbooks, 232 Madison Avenue,
Suite 1206, NY 10016, USA.

12 11 10 9 8 7 6 5 4

British Library Cataloguing in Publication Data
Daitz, Myrna
    Crafty ideas for parties.
    1.   Entertainments: Children's parties.
    I.   Title.   II. Chapman, Gillian.
    793.2'1

ISBN 1-85015-391-4

Series designer: Gillian Chapman.
Editorial: Margaret Montgomery.
Typeset by Brush Off Studios, St Albans, Herts AL3 4PH.
Printed in China.

CRAFTY
IDEAS FOR
PARTIES

Myrna Daitz

pictures by Gillian Chapman

Editor Margaret Montgomery

EXLEY
NEW YORK • WATFORD, UK

In the same series:

Contents

Introduction

Crafty Ideas for Parties contains over twenty-five projects designed to make parties more fun for young children of five to ten years. Children can now start to enjoy a party long before the guests arrive.

Most of the projects use ordinary materials found in every home – scrap paper, paints, scissors, glue, cardboard, felt tip pens and crayons. Very little will have to be specially bought in. The children will benefit from the early development of craft skills – using scissors, learning to fit and to measure things – as well as developing concentration.

Making things builds up a great deal of confidence in children. Nothing is worse than starting and failing at something, and this is doubly true for young children. Their first experience of crafting should bring a feeling of achievement and creation. So we have been very careful to test the projects. Our author, Myrna Daitz, is a schoolteacher with years of experience of craft teaching. She has also had help from other teachers in testing new ideas in the classroom.

Children should not worry if their completed projects don't look like the ones in the book. It is important that they feel free to be creative, and to enjoy the activities – the achievement comes not from slavishly copying ideas, but from inventing things. If their first attempts don't work out quite right, there's no terrible cost involved. They can start again, and have the thrill of seeing their next attempt improve before their eyes.

We have included a selection of creative, but safe, ideas for party food. Whenever an ingredient needs cooking, we have recommended it be shop bought or pre-cooked by an adult.

There's so much to do, so much to plan. Happy partying!

A Simple Invitation

1. On each sheet of paper write the details of your party – the date, time, place and whether it's fancy dress.

2. Decorate the invitations. For a theme party, decorate them to match – e.g. a treasure map for a pirate's party.

3. Roll up each invitation and hold it together with a piece of adhesive tape. For a pirate's party, tie the invitation with ribbon or string. For a Christmas party, put the invitations inside small cardboard tubes and decorate them to look like crackers.

What you need :-
Sheets of white paper.
Scissors.
Crayons or felt tip pens.
Ribbon or string.
Adhesive tape.

Prizes for the best-dressed Pirate!

Come
to my Pirate party
on - - - - - - - - - -
from - - - - - - - - - -
at - - - - - - - - - -
from The Captain
R.S.V.P.

N
W E
S   Look out for the Pirate flag↑

To Pirate Sue

Parent's Handy Hint :-
Make a Pirate Flag or tie balloons outside the front door on the day of the party.

A Monster Invitation

What you need :-
Thin cardboard.   Scissors.
A pencil.
Crayons or felt tip pens.
Silver paper or sequins.
Glue.
Writing paper.

1. Cut out a piece of thin cardboard 25cm x 17cm (10″ x 7″) and fold it in half.

2. Draw a monster on the front, then cut out the shape from both pieces of cardboard. Take care *not* to cut the folded left edge.

3. Using crayons or felt tip pens, make the monster look as scary as you can.

4. Glue on pieces of silver paper or sequins for eyes.

5. Write the details of your party on a piece of paper and glue it inside your card.

*   Give out the invitations at least two weeks before the party.

Come to my
MONSTER
party.
[dress scary!]

Adult's Handy Hint :-
Any character can be used for this invitation, depending on the theme of the party.

9

Pop-up Invitation

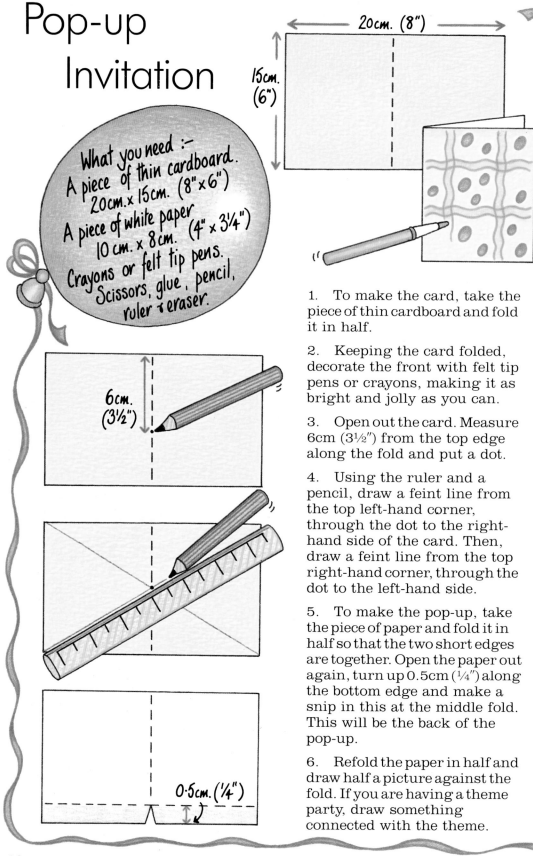

What you need :-
A piece of thin cardboard.
20cm. x 15cm. (8" x 6")
A piece of white paper
10 cm. x 8 cm. (4" x 3¼")
Crayons or felt tip pens.
Scissors, glue, pencil,
ruler & eraser.

20cm. (8")

15cm. (6")

6cm. (3½")

0.5cm. (¼")

1. To make the card, take the piece of thin cardboard and fold it in half.

2. Keeping the card folded, decorate the front with felt tip pens or crayons, making it as bright and jolly as you can.

3. Open out the card. Measure 6cm (3½") from the top edge along the fold and put a dot.

4. Using the ruler and a pencil, draw a feint line from the top left-hand corner, through the dot to the right-hand side of the card. Then, draw a feint line from the top right-hand corner, through the dot to the left-hand side.

5. To make the pop-up, take the piece of paper and fold it in half so that the two short edges are together. Open the paper out again, turn up 0.5cm (¼") along the bottom edge and make a snip in this at the middle fold. This will be the back of the pop-up.

6. Refold the paper in half and draw half a picture against the fold. If you are having a theme party, draw something connected with the theme.

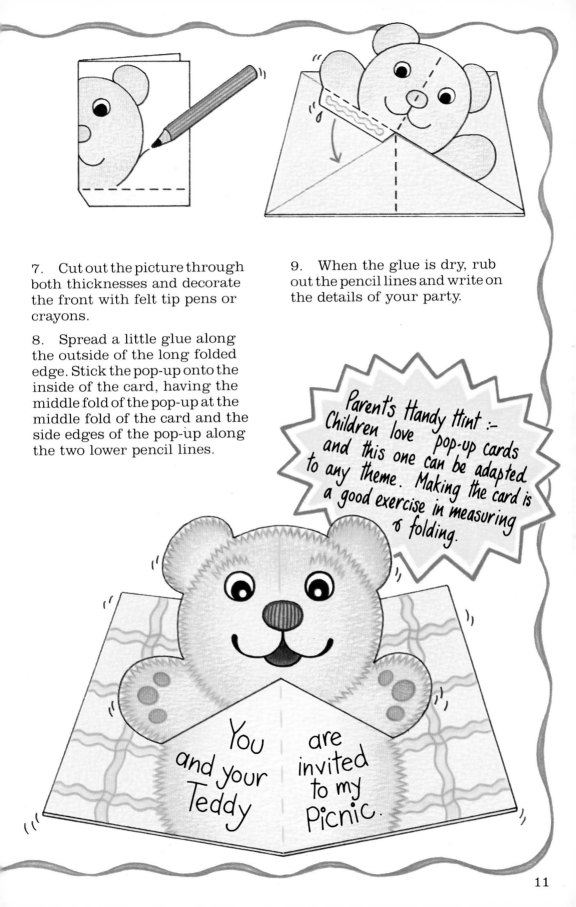

7. Cut out the picture through both thicknesses and decorate the front with felt tip pens or crayons.

8. Spread a little glue along the outside of the long folded edge. Stick the pop-up onto the inside of the card, having the middle fold of the pop-up at the middle fold of the card and the side edges of the pop-up along the two lower pencil lines.

9. When the glue is dry, rub out the pencil lines and write on the details of your party.

Parent's Handy Hint :- Children love pop-up cards and this one can be adapted to any theme. Making the card is a good exercise in measuring & folding.

You and your Teddy are invited to my picnic.

Place Cards

What you need :-
Pieces of thin cardboard.
Scissors.
Felt tip pens or crayons.
A pencil.
Glue.

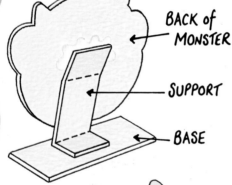

BACK of MONSTER
SUPPORT
BASE

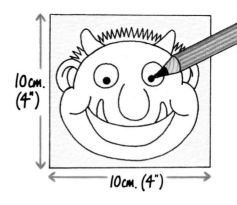

10cm. (4")
10cm. (4")

1. Cut out a piece of cardboard 10cm x 10cm (4" x 4").

2. Draw a picture of a monster on the cardboard and cut it out.

3. Decorate the monster with felt tip pens or crayons, leaving a space to write the guest's name.

4. Cut out another piece of cardboard 8cm x 6cm (3½" x 2½") to use for the base.

5. To make the support, cut out a strip of cardboard 6cm x 2cm (2½" x ¾").

6. Fold over 2cm (¾") at each end of the support and glue one end to the base and the other end to the back of the monster.

7. Make one card for each guest, then write the names on the front of the cards.

Jane

Parent's Handy Hint :-
A different monster can be used for each place card. Deciding where each guest will sit before the party starts will avoid unnecessary fuss when it's time to eat.

Party Straws

← 7cm. (3") →

1. Draw several different shaped faces on a piece of thin cardboard. Each one needs to be approximately 7cm (3") wide.

2. Decorate the faces with felt tip pens or crayons, but leave out the nose.

3. Carefully cut out the faces.

4. Fold each face in half, cut two slots in the middle across the fold and thread on to the straws.

FOLD

FOLD

Parent's Handy Hint :–
This is a simple way to brighten up plain straws.

13

Novelty Napkins

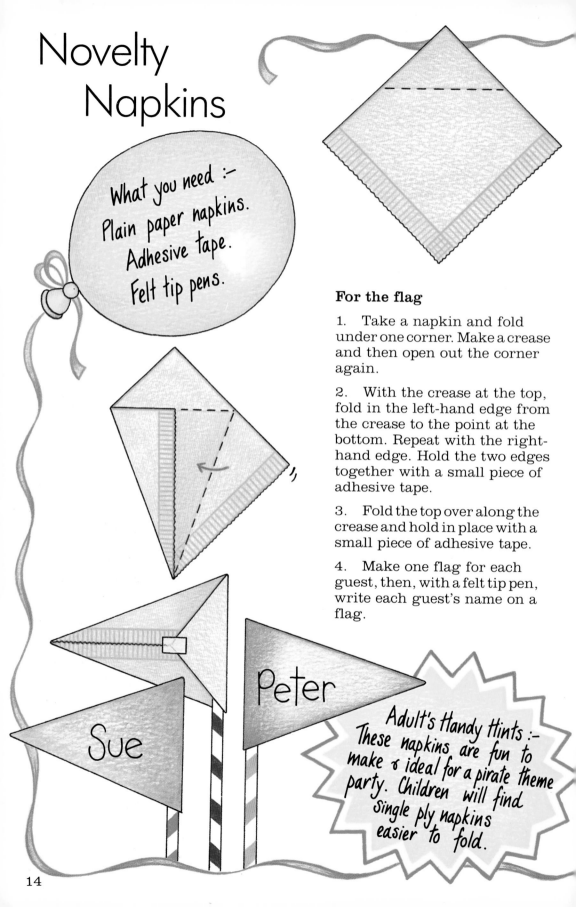

What you need :-
Plain paper napkins.
Adhesive tape.
Felt tip pens.

For the flag

1.   Take a napkin and fold under one corner. Make a crease and then open out the corner again.

2.   With the crease at the top, fold in the left-hand edge from the crease to the point at the bottom. Repeat with the right-hand edge. Hold the two edges together with a small piece of adhesive tape.

3.   Fold the top over along the crease and hold in place with a small piece of adhesive tape.

4.   Make one flag for each guest, then, with a felt tip pen, write each guest's name on a flag.

Peter

Sue

Adult's Handy Hints :-
These napkins are fun to make & ideal for a pirate theme party. Children will find single ply napkins easier to fold.

For the hat

1. Take a napkin and open it out completely. Turn in 4cm (1½") along the left-hand edge and the right-hand edge.

2. With the folded edges on the inside, fold the napkin in half from top to bottom.

3. Turn up 4cm (1½") along the bottom edge. Make a crease along the fold, then open the fold out again. Turn the napkin over and repeat on the other side.

4. Fold the napkin in half from side to side. Mark the middle on the crease along the bottom, then open out again.

5. Fold the top left-hand corner down to the mark on the crease. Repeat with the right-hand corner and then fold up the bottom edge along the crease.

6. Turn the napkin over. Fold up the bottom edge along the crease and write on the guest's name with a felt tip pen. If you are having a pirate theme party, give each guest a title – e.g. Pirate James, Captain Sue, Sailor Sam.

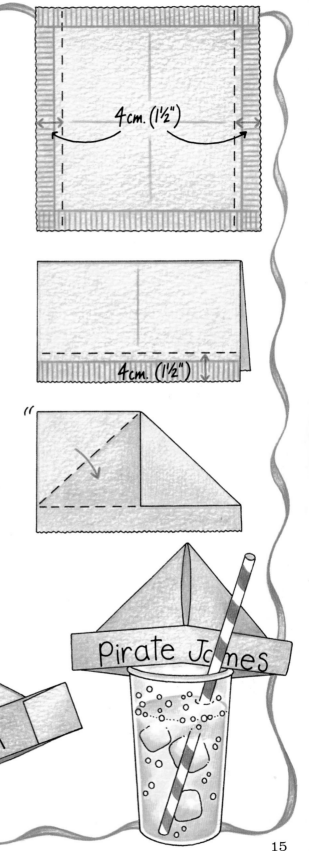

Disco Decorations

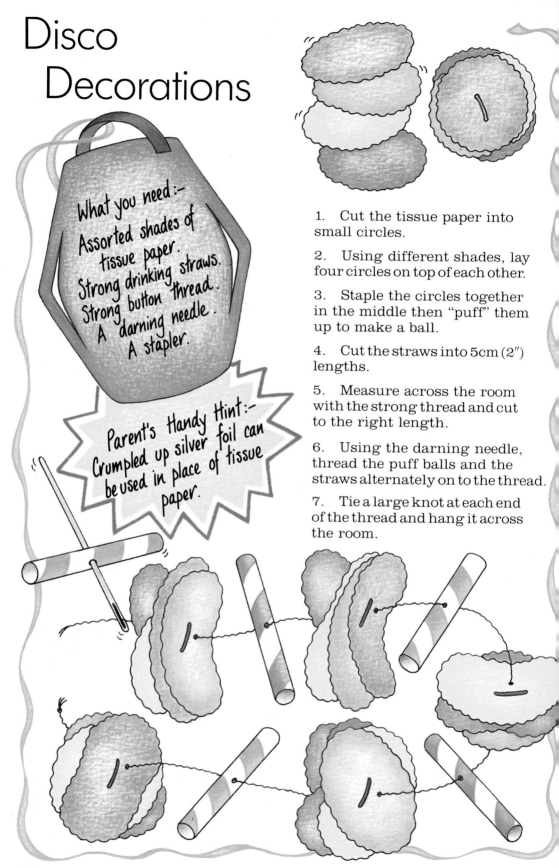

What you need :-
Assorted shades of tissue paper.
Strong drinking straws.
Strong button thread.
A darning needle.
A stapler.

Parent's Handy Hint :-
Crumpled up silver foil can be used in place of tissue paper.

1. Cut the tissue paper into small circles.

2. Using different shades, lay four circles on top of each other.

3. Staple the circles together in the middle then "puff" them up to make a ball.

4. Cut the straws into 5cm (2″) lengths.

5. Measure across the room with the strong thread and cut to the right length.

6. Using the darning needle, thread the puff balls and the straws alternately on to the thread.

7. Tie a large knot at each end of the thread and hang it across the room.

Paper Lanterns

What you need :-
Assorted shades of paper.
Scissors.
Glue.
Thick button thread.
Adhesive tape.

Adult's Handy Hint :-
Home made decorations are great fun and can keep children busy for hours.

1. For each lantern cut out a rectangle of paper 23cm x 15cm (9″ x 6″).

2. Fold the paper in half lengthways and cut strips along the folded edge. Take care *not* to cut right across the paper.

3. Open out the paper. Fold it round and glue one edge over the other.

4. To make a handle, cut out a small strip of paper. Stick each end to the top of the lantern with adhesive tape.

5. Thread all the finished lanterns evenly along the button thread, and hold them in place with a piece of adhesive tape. When they are all evenly spaced, hang the thread across the room.

Spooky Spiders

What you need :-
Cardboard egg box.
Scissors.   Glue.
Black paint & paint brush.
4 pipe cleaners.   Elastic.
    A sharp pencil.
    Buttons or sequins.

1. Cut up a cardboard egg box and use the hollow the egg sits in for the spider's body.

2. Paint the body black.

3. Paint four pipe cleaners black and when dry cut in half.

4. Using a sharp pencil, make four holes in each side of the body.

Adult's Handy Hints :-
Use a cardboard egg box because it is easier to paint. These scary spiders certainly make a party go with a swing!

5. Push each half pipe cleaner through a hole. Bend down approximately 1cm (½″) inside and turn up the ends to shape the feet.

6. Glue buttons or sequins on to the body for eyes.

7. Make a hole in the top of the body. Cut a piece of elastic and tie a knot at one end. Thread the elastic through the hole from the inside of the body.

8. Suspend the spider from the ceiling.

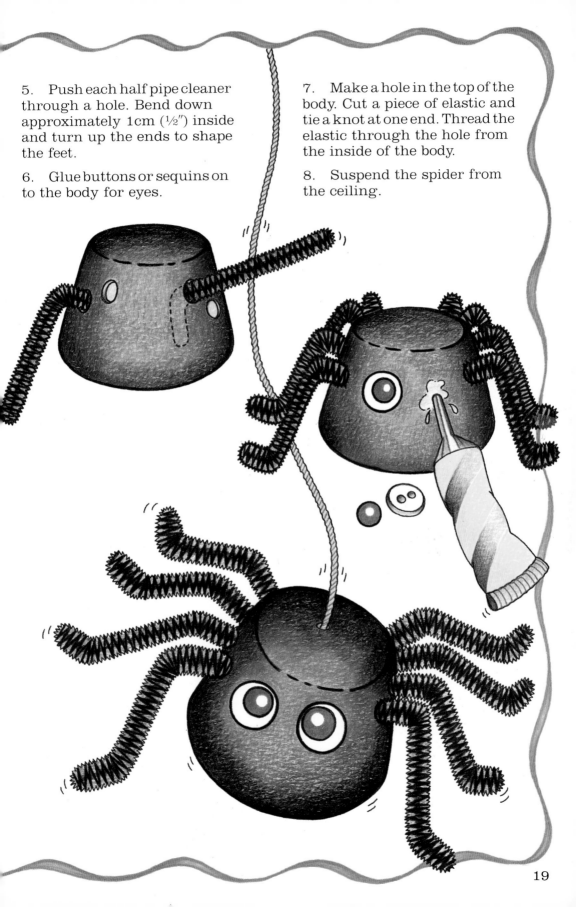

Party Masks

1. Place the tracing paper over the mask pattern and draw around the edge and around the eyes with a pencil.

2. Carefully cut out the mask from the tracing paper and use this for a template.

3. Place the template on the cardboard, draw around the edge and around the eyes. Cut out along the lines and make a hole at the top on each side.

What you need :-
Tracing paper.   Scissors.
Thin elastic.   Pencil.
Crayons or felt tip pens.
Glue & a brush.
Assorted shades of thin cardboard.
A selection of things to decorate the mask, e.g. tubes of glitter, sequins, straws, feathers, woollen yarn.

Mask template

holes for elastic

Parent's Handy Hint :-
Have the mask shapes cut out ready and let the party guests decorate them themselves.

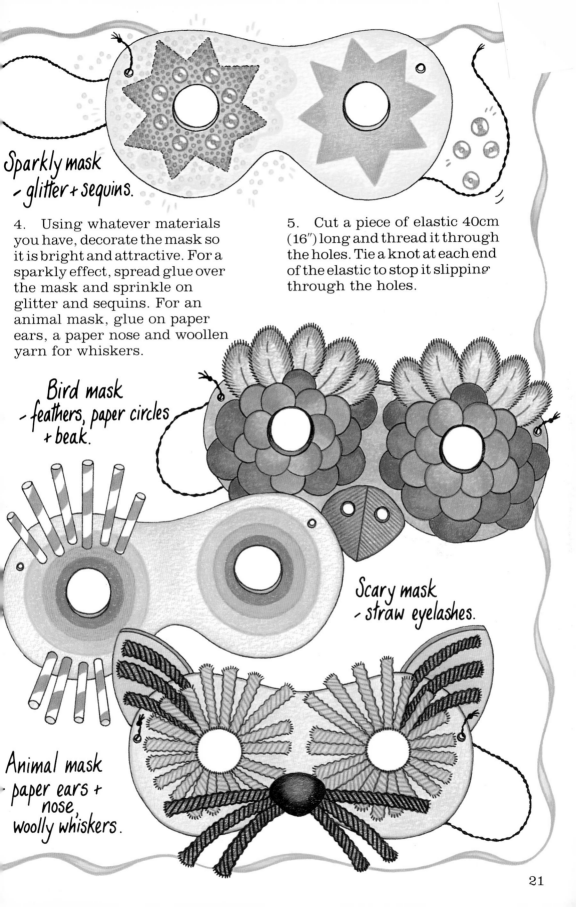

Sparkly mask
- glitter + sequins.

4. Using whatever materials you have, decorate the mask so it is bright and attractive. For a sparkly effect, spread glue over the mask and sprinkle on glitter and sequins. For an animal mask, glue on paper ears, a paper nose and woollen yarn for whiskers.

5. Cut a piece of elastic 40cm (16″) long and thread it through the holes. Tie a knot at each end of the elastic to stop it slipping through the holes.

Bird mask
- feathers, paper circles + beak.

Scary mask
- straw eyelashes.

Animal mask
- paper ears + nose, woolly whiskers.

Clown's Hat

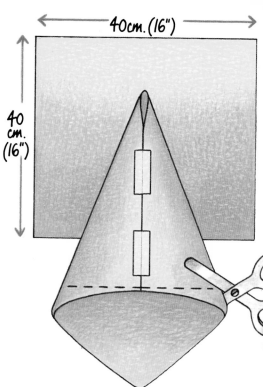

What you need :—
A large piece of paper.
Ruler.   Scissors.
Pencil.
Adhesive tape.
Glue or a brush.
Tissue paper.
Tinsel.

1.   Cut out a piece of paper 40cm x 40cm (16″ x 16″).

2.   Fold the paper round to form a cone. Overlap the edges and hold them together with adhesive tape. Trim the bottom edge so that it is straight.

3.   To make the pom-poms, crumple up pieces of tissue paper and glue them to the front of the hat.

4.   Cut a piece of tinsel to fit around the bottom edge of the hat and glue it on.

Parent's Handy Hint :—
This hat can also be used as a witch's or wizard's hat by using black paper or decorating it with pieces of silver foil.

Monster's Hat

What you need :-
1 round, plastic food container, 15cm. (6") across.
Crepe paper.   Glue.
Silver foil.
3 ping-pong balls.
Thin elastic.   Adhesive
A felt tip pen.   tape.

Parent's Handy Hint:- Always keep empty food containers — they are extremely useful for craft projects.

1. Make sure the container has been washed thoroughly.

2. Cut a piece of crêpe paper to measure 36cm x 36cm (14" x 14").

3. Stand the container in the middle of the paper. Wrap the paper over the edges and hold it inside with pieces of adhesive tape.

4. For the eyes, use a felt tip pen to draw a circle on each of the ping-pong balls. Cut three pieces of elastic. Using adhesive tape, stick one end of each piece of elastic to a ping-pong ball and the other end to the container.

5. To make the hair, cut out 0.5cm (½") wide strips of silver foil and glue these all around the container.

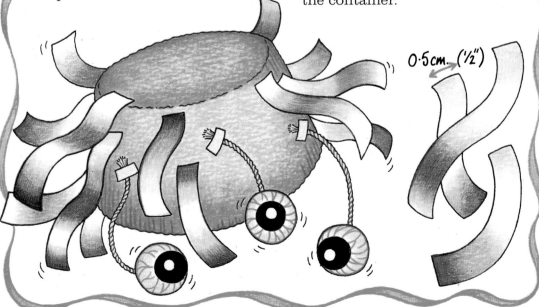

0.5cm. (½")

Pirate's Party Hat

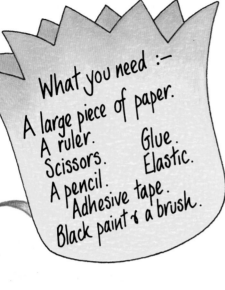

What you need :-
A large piece of paper.
A ruler.
Scissors.   Glue.
A pencil.   Elastic.
Adhesive tape.
Black paint & a brush.

Adult's Handy Hint :-
These quick & easy hats can be made out of newspaper if you don't have any large sheets of plain paper.

1.   Cut the paper to measure 45cm x 30cm (18″ x 12″).

2.   Lay the paper on a flat surface and fold the paper in half.

3.   With the folded edge away from you draw a line across 8cm (3″) up from the bottom edge. Measure 15cm (6″) across this line and put a mark. This is the middle.

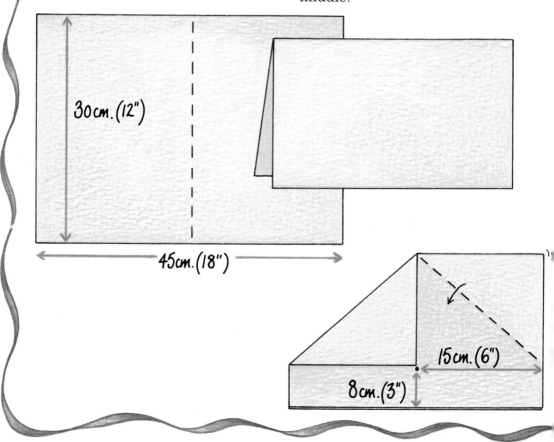

30cm. (12″)

45cm. (18″)

15cm. (6″)

8cm. (3″)

4. Fold in the two top corners so that they meet exactly in the middle of the line.

5. Fold the bottom flap up and turn the hat over. Turn up the remaining flap. Tuck in the four corners and use pieces of adhesive tape to hold them together. Paint the hat black.

6. Cut out a circle 8cm (3″) across from the left-over paper. Draw a skull and crossbones on the circle and glue to the front of the hat.

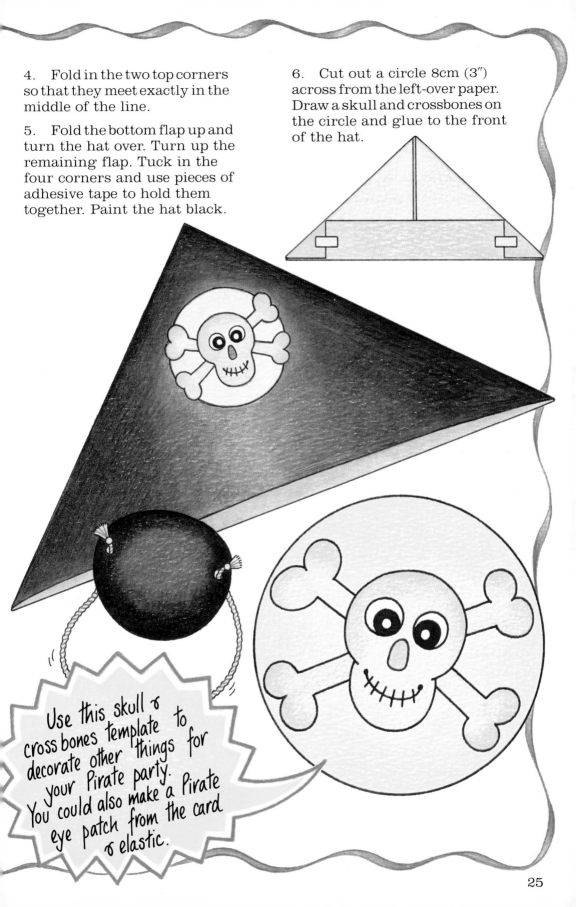

Use this skull & cross bones template to decorate other things for your Pirate party. You could also make a Pirate eye patch from the card & elastic.

Fancy Crackers

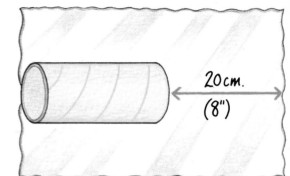

20cm.
(8")

1.   Cut a piece of foil to measure 20cm (8") longer than the toilet roll tube.

2.   Roll the foil several times around the tube, leaving 10cm (4") spare at each end of the tube. Seal with adhesive tape.

3.   Very carefully twist the foil at one end and tie it with the thread.

4.   Put a present in the cracker at the other end. Write a joke on a piece of paper and put that in as well.

5.   Close the cracker by twisting the foil at the open end and tying with thread.

6.   Snip the foil at both ends of the cracker up to the cotton thread to make fancy ends.

Adult's Handy Hints :-
These crackers are so much cheaper than bought ones & look lovely on the table. They can be decorated with gummed paper shapes.

Sparkly Badges

What you need :-
Thin cardboard. Glue.
Tubes of glitter.
Assorted bright gummed paper.
Scissors. Safety pins.
Adhesive tape.
Paint brush.
Newspaper.

1. Cut out different shapes from the cardboard – circles, triangles, stars. You'll need one shape for each party guest.

2. Cut the same shapes out of gummed paper and use these to cover the cardboard.

3. Using the glue and paintbrush, carefully make a design on the gummed paper.

4. Lay the badges on the newspaper and sprinkle glitter over the glue design. Gently tap the back of the badge to remove the excess glitter.

5. Using a small piece of adhesive tape, attach one side of a safety pin to the back of each badge.

Parent's Handy Hints :-
Personalized badges can be made by putting each guest's initial on a badge. If you are having a theme party, the designs can be linked to the theme.

Crazy Costumes

What you need :-
Sheets of newspaper or other large sheets of paper.
Empty food packets, paper bags or cups, cardboard tubes, silver foil, scraps of fabric.
Scissors, adhesive tape.
Glue.

1. Set out all the materials on a table before the guests arrive.

2. Ask the guests to stand around the table and set a time limit for them to create a costume they can wear using the various materials.

3. When the time is up, the children vote for the costume they like best. The child who gets the most votes is the winner.

Adult's Handy Hint :-
Have this competition at the beginning of the party, then the children can wear their costumes for the rest of the time.

If you are holding a theme party have materials to match!

Mad Monster Cake

What you need :-
1 sponge flan case.
1 can of fruit purée.
2 ring doughnuts.
Chocolate sauce.
2 cherries.
Chopped nuts.
Toothpicks.

Parent's Handy Hint :-
You can buy sponge flan cases ready made. This is a super cake for a monster theme party!

1. Pour the fruit purée into the flan case. Spread it out evenly so that all the sponge is covered.

2. Take the doughnut rings and carefully cut them in half. You now have four semi-circles.

3. To make the monster's humps, stand three semi-circles in the purée.

4. To make the monster's neck and head, cut the remaining semi-circle in half and put one piece at the end of the humps.

5. To finish the monster, put the cherries on the toothpicks and stick these into the monster's head for eyes. Dribble chocolate sauce over the humps and sprinkle with chopped nuts.

Chocolate Galleon

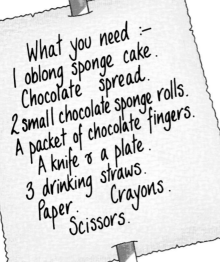

What you need :-
1 oblong sponge cake.
Chocolate spread.
2 small chocolate sponge rolls.
A packet of chocolate fingers.
A knife & a plate.
3 drinking straws.
Crayons.
Paper.
Scissors.

1.   Put the sponge cake on a plate and carefully cover it with a layer of chocolate spread.

2.   Place chocolate fingers side-by-side all around the cake.

3.   On top of the cake, place two chocolate rolls at one end and three chocolate fingers along each side for oars.

Adult's Handy Hint :-
All the ingredients for this cake can be bought ready-made — it will go down well at a pirates party!

4. To make the flags, cut out three rectangles 7cm x 5cm (3″ x 2″) and three triangles from the paper.

5. Decorate the flags.

6. Cut two slits through each of the rectangular flags and slide one on to each straw. Cut a slit at the top of each straw to hold the triangular flags.

7. To finish, carefully push the straws into the top of the cake.

7cm. (3″)

5cm. (2″)

LOOK FOR THE SKULL & CROSS BONES TEMPLATE ON p.25.

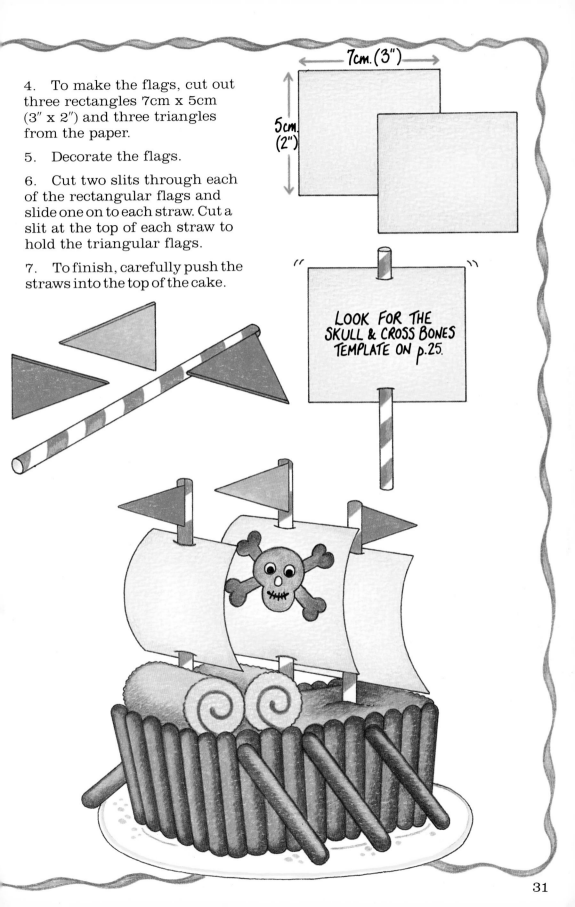

Monster Slime

What you need :-
Equal amounts of orange juice, blackcurrant juice & diet cola.
Blackcurrant jelly cubes.
A large bowl.

1. Cut the jelly cubes into small pieces and place in a bowl.

2. Pour the blackcurrant juice, orange juice and cola into the bowl and stir well.

Parent's Handy Hint:-
Even though this drink looks like blood, it is really quite nutritious!

Party Punch

What you need :–
Fresh orange juice.
Seedless grapes.
An apple.
A can of mandarin segments
in fruit juice.
Ice cubes.
Large bowl.
Sprigs of fresh mint.

1. Wash and dry the grapes.

2. Wash the apple and divide into quarters. Remove the core and cut the apple into thin slices.

3. Put the apple slices and grapes into the bowl and add the mandarin segments and juice.

4. Pour the orange juice over the fruit and stir gently.

5. Add the ice cubes and float the mint leaves on the top for decoration.

Adult's Handy Hint :–
Help may be needed slicing the apple. Any type of fruit can be used & sparkling lemonade can be added.

Salad Sailing Boats

What you need :–
Cucumber.
Celery.
Tomatoes.
A selection of fillings.
Lettuce.
A sheet of white paper.
Paints or felt tip pens.
Toothpicks.
Scissors.

8cm. (3")

1. Cut the cucumber and celery into pieces 8cm (3") long. Cut the cucumber pieces in half and scoop out the seeds.

2. Cut a slice off the top of the tomatoes and scoop out the seeds.

3. To stop the "boats" falling over, cut a very thin slice off the bottom of each tomato and of each piece of cucumber and celery.

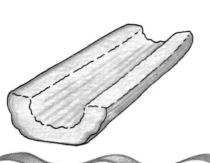

Parent's Handy Hint :–
Help may be needed to scoop out the cucumber or tomato seeds.

mashed sardines with lemon juice.

grated cheese & chopped pineapple.

cottage cheese & chives.

4. Prepare the fillings and spoon into the boats.

5. To make the sails, cut out triangles from the paper and decorate with paints or felt tip pens.

6. Thread a toothpick through each sail and stick one into each boat.

7. Wash and dry the lettuce, put on a plate and arrange the boats on the "sea" of lettuce.

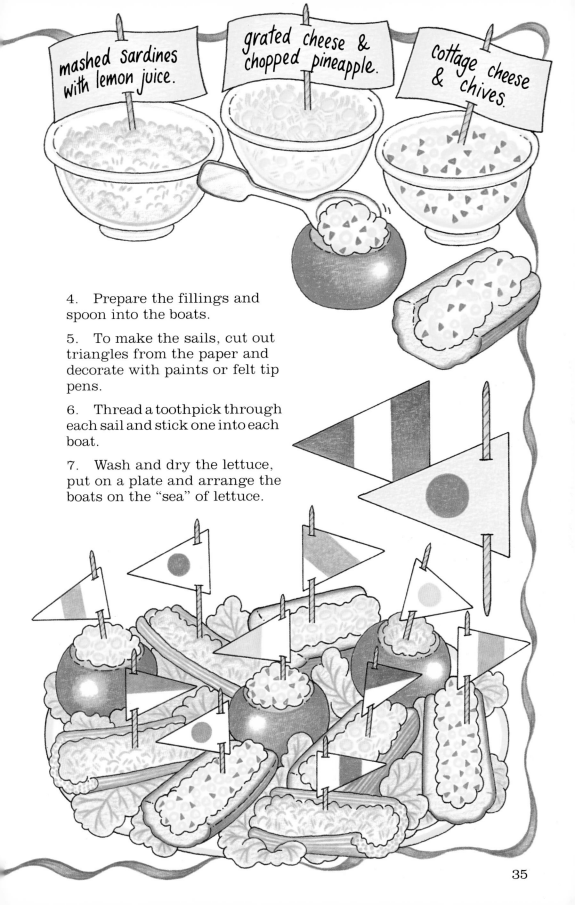

Wagonwheels

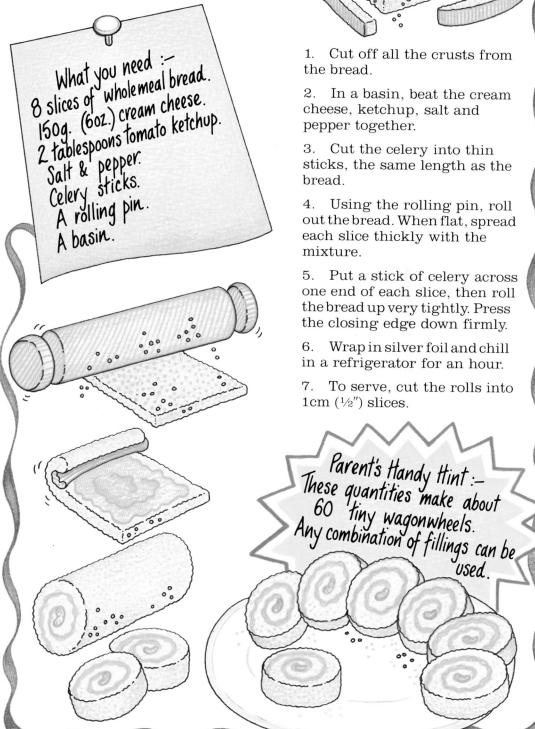

What you need :-
8 slices of wholemeal bread.
150g. (6oz.) cream cheese.
2 tablespoons tomato ketchup.
Salt & pepper.
Celery sticks.
A rolling pin.
A basin.

1. Cut off all the crusts from the bread.

2. In a basin, beat the cream cheese, ketchup, salt and pepper together.

3. Cut the celery into thin sticks, the same length as the bread.

4. Using the rolling pin, roll out the bread. When flat, spread each slice thickly with the mixture.

5. Put a stick of celery across one end of each slice, then roll the bread up very tightly. Press the closing edge down firmly.

6. Wrap in silver foil and chill in a refrigerator for an hour.

7. To serve, cut the rolls into 1cm (½″) slices.

Parent's Handy Hint :-
These quantities make about 60 tiny wagonwheels. Any combination of fillings can be used.

Jolly Roger Jellies

What you need :-
1 packet of jelly.
150 ml. (5 fl. oz.) whipping cream.
Cherries.
Grated chocolate or chopped nuts.
1 chocolate finger.
Chocolate drops.
A licorice strip.

Parent's Handy Hint :-

Supervise your child making the jelly with the hot water.

1.   Make the jelly according to the instructions on the packet. Pour into a round, shallow dish and put into a refrigerator to set.

2.   Whip the cream until it is stiff.

3.   When the jelly has set, spread the whipped cream over the top of it. Make a jolly face using the grated chocolate or chopped nuts for the hair and beard, chocolate drops for the eyes, a piece of chocolate finger for the nose and pieces of cherry for the mouth.

4.   To make the eye patch, sprinkle grated chocolate over one eye and add strips of licorice for "elastic".

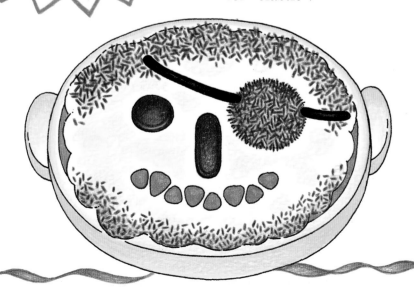

Clown Skittles

Parent's Handy Hints :-
This is a great way of using up empty drink bottles. The game allows children to be creative & helps improve counting skills.

What you need :-
6 empty clear plastic drink bottles. Glue.
Assorted gummed paper.
Bright adhesive tape.
Double-sided adhesive tape.
6 small plain paper plates.
Felt tip pens or crayons.
Tubes of glitter.
Soft ball.

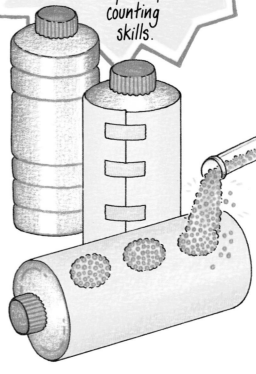

1. Make sure all the bottles have been washed thoroughly.

2. Remove the labels and decorate the bottles using the gummed paper, adhesive tape, and glitter. Make them look as bright as possible.

3. Using crayons or felt tip pens, draw a clown's face on the paper plates. Instead of a nose, give each plate a number.

4. Using a piece of double-sided adhesive tape, attach a plate to the top of each bottle, so the plate covers the neck of the bottle.

5. Stand the clown skittles in a group and take turns to roll the ball at them. Add up the numbers on the knocked-down skittles. Set a target of fifty and the first player to reach the target is the winner.

Clown skittles can be played indoors or outdoors.

ishing for Presents

Use this shape for your fish.

What you need :-
A large cardboard carton.
Sheets of bright paper.
Wrapping paper & string.
One present for each guest.
Some booby prizes, e.g. an old sock,
Some pebbles, a lid.
Felt tip pens.
A small hook.
Glue & a brush.
A bamboo cane.
Scissors.
Thread.

1. Cut the flaps off the carton. Cut out pieces of paper to fit the sides of the carton and glue in place.

2. Cut out some fish shapes, glue these on to the sides then draw on some plants and seaweed using a felt tip pen.

3. To make the fishing rod, cut a length of thread and tie one end to the hook and the other end to the cane.

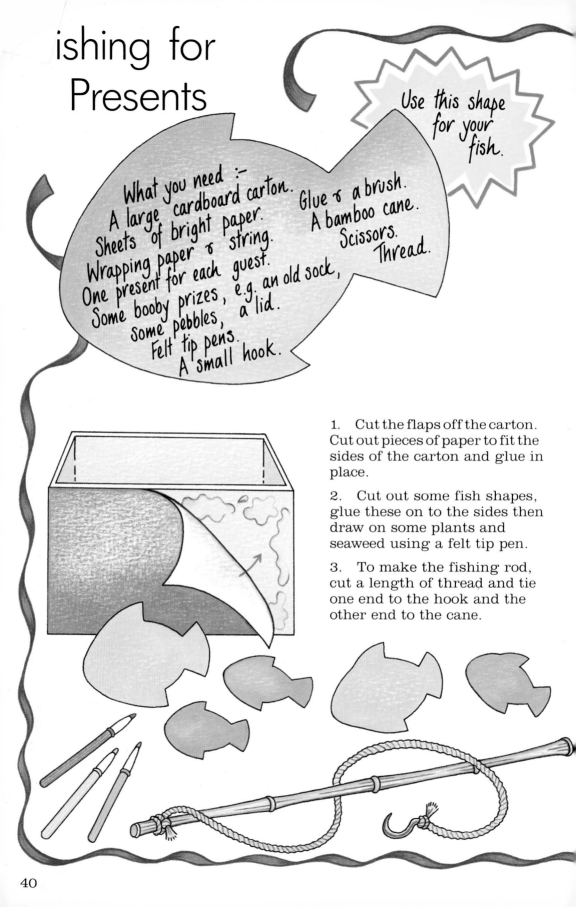

4. Wrap up the presents and the booby prizes. Tie each one with string, making a loop for the hook to catch on.

5. Put all the presents in the carton.

6. Each guest takes a turn to "fish" for a present. Anyone getting a booby prize has another turn.

Adult's Handy Hint:— The guests have great fun fishing for their presents. Wrap up small presents in large boxes to defeat greedy guests!

the Tail
on the Donkey

1. Draw a large picture of a donkey on the white paper.

2. Fix the picture to the wall using blu-tack so that you don't damage the surface.

3. To make the tail, cut out strips of crêpe paper and tie them together at one end with adhesive tape. On one side of the tape, put a piece of blu-tack to use for sticking the tail on to the donkey.

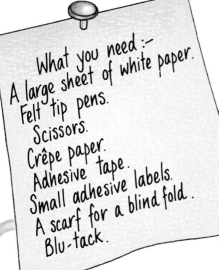

What you need :-
A large sheet of white paper.
Felt tip pens.
Scissors.
Crêpe paper.
Adhesive tape.
Small adhesive labels.
A scarf for a blind fold.
Blu-tack.

4. To play the game: Each player has a turn. The player whose turn it is puts on the blindfold and is spun round gently three or four times. The player is faced in front of the donkey and given the tail to place on it. Write the player's name on an adhesive label and stick this to the place where the tail was put. When each child has had a turn, the one who put the tail closest to the donkey's bottom is the winner.

Parent's Handy Hints :-
The picture can be adapted for any theme party – e.g. the patch on the pirate, the hat on the witch, the nose on the monster.

Tambourine

1. Cut strips of crêpe paper 0.5cm (½") wide and 30cm (12") long. Using adhesive tape, stick one end of each strip around the inside edge of one pie dish.

2. Put some dried peas or dried beans in the same pie dish, then cover it with the other dish.

3. Staple around the edges of the two dishes to hold them together.

4. Stand the dishes on a sheet of paper and, using the glue and paintbrush, make a design on one of the dishes. Sprinkle glitter over the design then tap the dish to remove the excess. Leave to dry then decorate the other side in the same way.

Parent's Handy Hint :-
NEVER let children play with cans that have rough edges. If you can't stand the noise, give them out just before the party ends!

Musical Cans

For the blower

1. Decorate the can with bands of bright adhesive tape.

2. Take two straws and tape them together 5cm (2") from one end.

3. Place the other end of the straws right next to the hole in the top of the can. Hold them in place with adhesive tape.

4. Blow down the straws to get a hooting noise.

For the shaker

1. Put some dried peas, dried beans or pieces of crumpled-up foil into an empty can.

2. Cover the top of the can with strips of adhesive tape, allowing them to overlap the edges of the can. Turn the can over and cover the bottom in the same way.

3. Decorate the outside of the can with different shades of bright adhesive tape.

4. Shake the can about to get the sound of maracas.

A Drum

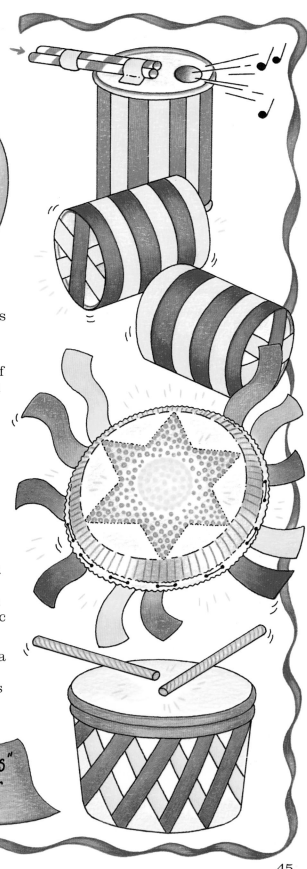

1. Make sure the container has been washed and dried thoroughly.

2. Use the different shades of adhesive tape to make a pattern on the outside of the container.

3. Lay the piece of plastic on a flat surface and stand the container upside down on it.

4. Draw a circle around the container, making it approximately 4cm (1½″) bigger than the container.

5. Cut out the circle and use it to cover the top of the container. Smooth it out so that there aren't any wrinkles in it, then hold it in place with the elastic band.

6. To finish the drum, stick a piece of wide adhesive tape around the top to hide the edges of the plastic and the elastic band.

Have enough "instruments" so that there is one for each guest!

Treasure Island

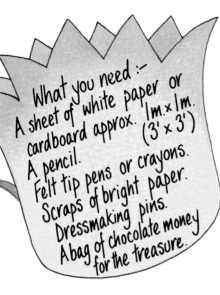

What you need :-
A sheet of white paper or
cardboard approx. 1m × 1m.
(3' × 3')
A pencil.
Felt tip pens or crayons.
Scraps of bright paper.
Dressmaking pins.
A bag of chocolate money
for the treasure.

1. Draw a large map of an island on the paper or cardboard.

2. Using felt tip pens or crayons, put some detail on the map – trees, rivers, huts, footpaths. Then add some place names, like Pirates Cove, Bounty Bay, Crossbone Wood.

3. Turn the map over, and put a cross somewhere to show where the "treasure" is buried.

4. Cut out a small flag for each guest from the scrap paper. Write the guests' names on the flags. Attach a pin to each flag.

5. Pin the map to a board, or lay it on the floor, and ask each guest in turn to stick their flag into the map.

6. When everyone has had their turn, turn the map over. Whoever has stuck their flag closest to the cross is the winner and gets the "treasure".

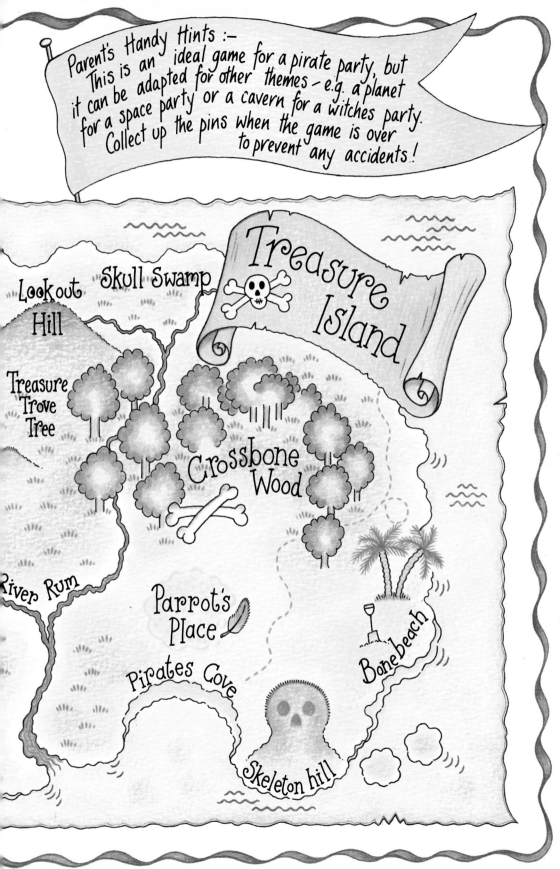